Gambler's Guide to the Stock Market

7 Winning Retirement Planning Investment Strategies for Your 401k, Traditional IRA and Roth IRA.

Lincoln T. James

Edition License Notes

ISBN-13: 978-1511508377

ISBN-10: 151150837X

Library of Congress Control Number: 2015908476

CreateSpace Independent Publishing Platform, North Charleston, SC

Printed in the United States of America

10 9 8 7 6 5 4 3 2 1

To my loving wife, without whose help and support this book would not have been possible.
~LTJ

Author Note

Gambler's Guide to the Stock Market is self-published. I hope you find the information useful. If you like the book I would love to hear your feedback. Please leave me a review for the book on Amazon.com.

http://amzn.to/1HcMGhE

Thanks for taking the time to read the book.

    ~ Lincoln T. James

Contents

Disclaimer

Investors should be cautious about any and all stock recommendations and should consider the source of any advice on stock selection. Remember personal or corporate ownership may influence or factor into an expert's stock analysis or opinion. Some people have an agenda or a personal stake in equities they recommend.

All investors are advised to conduct their own independent research into individual stocks before making a decision to purchase equities. In addition, investors are advised that past stock performance is no guarantee of future price appreciation.

The reader acknowledges and agrees that, to the fullest extent permitted by law, neither the author, Gambler's Guide to the Stock Market, Reluctant Bull, LTK Enterprises, LLC nor their suppliers shall be liable for any loss of business or profits nor any direct, indirect or consequential loss or damage resulting from any omission, irregularity, inaccuracy or use of this information.

Reader agrees to assume all risk resulting from the application of any of the information found herein. Gambler's Guide to the Stock Market, Reluctant Bull, LTK Enterprises, LLC, and the author does not accept any liability for any loss or damage whatsoever caused in reliance upon such information and no information provided here is to be interpreted as a suggestion to buy, sell or hold securities. This book is for educational / informational purposes only, and in no way guarantees your profitability in the stock market. There is no guarantee that you will earn any money using the techniques and ideas presented here.

Reader agrees to indemnify and hold harmless Gambler's Guide to the Stock Market, Reluctant Bull, LTK Enterprises, LLC and the author from and against any damages, costs and expenses, including any legal fees, potentially resulting from the application of any of the information provided by Gambler's Guide to the Stock Market, Reluctant Bull, LTK Enterprises, LLC and the author. This disclaimer applies to any damages, injury or loss caused by the use and application, whether directly or indirectly, of any advice or information presented, whether for breach of contract, tort, negligence, personal injury, criminal intent or under any other cause of action.

Conduct Your Own Due Diligence

Our content is for informational / educational purposes only. It is very important to do your own research and conduct your own due diligence before making any investment based on your own personal financial circumstances. You should seek financial advice from a trusted professional in connection with, or independently research and verify, any information that you find here and wish to rely upon, whether for the purpose of making an investment decision or otherwise. All information contained herein should be independently verified and confirmed.

No Investment Advice

Gambler's Guide to the Stock Market is not an investment adviser, we have no access to non-public information about publicly traded companies, and we do not give or receive financial advice, advice concerning investment decisions, tax nor legal advice. This book is for educational purposes and generic information related to stocks, investments and strategies. No content constitutes - or should be understood as constituting - a recommendation to enter into any securities transactions or to engage in any of the investment strategies presented here. We do not provide personalized recommendations or views as to whether a stock or investment approach is suited to the financial needs of a specific individual.

Accordingly, we will not be liable, whether in contract, tort (including negligence) or otherwise, in respect of any damage, expense or other loss you may suffer arising out of such information or any reliance you may place upon such information. Any arrangements between you and any third party are at your sole risk.

Caution

Be advised of the following important investment warnings.

*** The value of shares go down as well as up.

*** Never invest what you cannot afford to lose.

*** Past performance is not a guide to future performance.

Caveat Emptor! (For those who do not speak Latin: Buyer Beware.)

Who Do You Listen To?

Who Has Your Ear?

Whether you are used to hedging your bets, playing the odds, tossing a dart, flipping a coin or crunching the numbers, there are a few things you need to know to profitably navigate the wildly fluctuating, ill-tempered, torrid or deceptively peaceful waters of the stock market.

One thing is certain: changes are frequent, fast, and fluid. The market is fickle at best and often a perplexing riddle. Numerous and confusing economic factors, geopolitical turmoil, investor sentiments and human behavior all affect market timing, equity valuations, and the often times completely overwhelming world of statistical securities analysis. Unless of course you know a few key strategies and facts, you might find yourself adrift, without a paddle, up that well known stinking creek.

The goal of this book is to help you learn to successfully explore the world of the stock market, the factors that come into play in evaluating the markets, and to help the individual investor to think and decide on the best successful retirement planning investment strategies for themselves in both a 401k and / or an IRA (Traditional IRA or ROTH IRA). The goal is to provide an alternative view to the "expert's" opinions.

Experts in General

What is an expert? Here are a just a few examples of experts at work. In George Washington's day blood letting and leeches were routinely used by the so called medical experts of the day. Hand washing was once deemed an unnecessary waste of time. The founder of Digital Equipment Corporation also known as DEC, Ken Olsen, once said "There is no reason for an individual to have a computer in his home." Michael Dell, founder of Dell Computing, while speaking of Apple on October 6th, 1997 said "I'd shut it down and give the money back to the shareholders." Bill Gates, the founder of Microsoft, predicted in 2004 "2 years from now, spam would be solved." A Corporate executive for Decca Recording Company turned down the Beatles in 1962 saying "We don't like their sound. Groups of guitars are on the way out."

I don't know about you, but while listening to my collection of the Beatles, on my IPod, playing through my home computer's speakers, I routinely filter through my email box which continues to be overrun and clogged with spam. The only time I use leeches is when I go fishing and hand washing remains the back bone of good hygiene and disease prevention.

Market Experts

More pertinent to our discussion of the stock market and it's experts, John Maynard Keynes, widely considered to be one of the founders of modern macroeconomics and the most influential economist of the 20th century whose ideas are the basis for the school of thought known as Keynesian economics, said in 1927, 2 years before the worst financial crash in the history of the stock market, "We will not have any more crashes in our time." E. H. H. Simmons, President, New York Stock Exchange, January 12, 1928 said "I cannot help but raise a dissenting voice to statements that we are living in a fool's paradise, and that prosperity in this country must necessarily diminish and recede in the near future." Irving Fisher, professor of economics at Yale University, on October 17, 1929 said "Stocks have reached what looks like a permanently high plateau."

My Point

So much for expert opinions. Much of the time they are just passionately pontificating their agenda or what they "feel" will happen based on their many years of experience. Lots of times their opinions are nothing more than hot air or an educated guess at best.

The "experts" have always, and will continue to espouse ideas that may or may not be true, valid or even based in reality. Think of Bernie Madoff, Enron, Worldcom, Freddie Mac and Lehman Brothers to name just a few. People have agendas motivated by personal gain. Trust is a concept the "experts," sales people, con men, and sociopaths will always bend to their advantage. People, especially the so called experts, will always try and convince or brow beat you to their way of thinking. The free ebook you just downloaded the other day was provided to you by an author that has an agenda, more than likely motivated by personal gain. He may want you as a client. He may be offering consulting services, products for sale, software to make your life easier, some get rich quick scheme, snake oil... And all at a cost. The list is endless. You need to learn to evaluate opportunities for yourself.

Research, due diligence, home work, whatever you like to call it is your best friend and being knowledgeable about with whom, how, and where you put your money will in the long run forever be your best opportunity to maximize your returns on your investments. Remember, no one will watch your money like you will, and if you need proof of that one, check out how many former athletes, celebrities, and lottery winners have been bilked out of their fortunes. If investment brokers were so good at picking winners they would be trading their own accounts, not yours. Caveat Emptor!

The strategies presented here are for use in your retirement accounts, either a 401k, self-directed IRA (traditional IRA, or ROTH IRA.) Due to the possible tax implications, individual equity or other security purchases within a taxable account are beyond the scope of this book.

Before We Start

*** Before we go on to the strategies, unless otherwise stated, the investment vehicle we will be using is the S&P 500 represented in your 401k as the large cap index fund and available in your self-directed IRA as the Exchange Traded Fund (ETF) with the ticker symbol SPY.

Please be aware that when I reference SPY and SPX they are both the same except that SPY is the Exchange Traded Fund you will be purchasing in your accounts and SPX is the ticker symbol for the S&P 500.

In my opinion you would do well to have both a 401k and a self-directed IRA. I have several reasons for having both types of accounts. First, diversification is a good thing. Second, we can't know what the future will be. Quite simply, no one can predict how in the future the government will treat the taxation of one type of account versus the other. Third, regulations governing IRAs and 401ks could change. For example, as of this writing in 2015,

401ks are protected from bankruptcy however IRAs are not. While I strongly recommend that you have both types of accounts, I definitely recommended that you first fund the 401k account to gain your matching employer benefit before you fund your IRA.

You can visit my website Reluctantbull.com and sign up for free strategy updates and recommendations too.

http://bit.ly/reluctantbull

Who Wins and Why?

Who are you?

The professional gambler will always seek to bet or wager strategically by finding an edge and through sound money management maximize their returns.

Risk, reward, and payoff are concepts that the professionals constantly consider. What the professional gambler does is actually quite boring. If you are engaged in gambling where your heart is racing you are thrill seeking. This is a big red flag, and will affect your returns in a negative way.

When the professional considers risk, he will make calculated wagers or bets, where his odds are favorable and his risk of loss is mitigated, as much as possible. You would never recognize a professional gambler. He doesn't stick out from the crowd and he is not the charismatic figure from fiction books that you might picture. He operates from as many facts as he can garner and will use the odds to his advantage while limiting his exposure to risk. He is not the wild flamboyant trader throwing money around like it is confetti. Those people only exist in the movies and if you have a money / asset management professional working with you that gets his adrenalin rush from trading other people's accounts you need to switch immediately. Approaching money management with the mindset that it is entertaining or a thrill seeking adventure is a sure way to crash and burn and you don't want anyone in charge of your hard earned dollars with that mindset.

You will never find a professional gambler risking his capital on a game of chance where skill has no bearing. When you evaluate a game of chance, consider luck and skill. If you can loose on purpose there is a skill involved. If you are playing a game where you cannot loose on purpose that game is completely random and not something that you will find a professional engaged in. As an example, it makes no difference how much skill you have when playing roulette. The wheel will spin, and the ball will land where it lands, and you are simply gambling. No skill involved. Pure luck.

I had a former boss who claimed, in the game of Keno, that he could look at the numbers and somehow magically sense a pattern, and he would bet accordingly. The last I heard his mansion purchase was still on hold due to lack of funds. The most frightening thing about his "claimed" power was that my co-workers did indeed believe that he possessed that talent.

The Players.

Let's Meet a Few

of the Professionals.

The Card Counter

Card counting is a skill that provides the professional gambler with a mathematical edge over the casino. Card counters are found at the Black Jack table. Each hand that is dealt depletes the deck of certain cards and the card counter can then determine if the deck is rich, and has a higher than normal ratio of tens and aces remaining, making the deck player favorable and ripe for larger wagers. When the ratio falls the other way and the deck has a higher percentage of twos through sixes the card counter will wager as small as possible or leave the table.

The most well know and skilled at card counting will be banned from the casinos. Card counting can be so lucrative that a skilled card counter may even resort to disguises to keep from being recognized. While casinos will ban card counters, card counting is in no way, shape, or form illegal. The casino simply realizes that the card counter has a mathematical edge and can capitalize on it to the casino's disadvantage, and loss of money, sometimes huge sums of money. The casino is profitable only because the house always has an edge and to allow an entity into the casino that reduces that edge is completely unprofitable and risky. Hence the ban.

The Horse Race Handicapper

The professional handicapper thinks in probabilities and knows that the track requires the majority of bettors to lose, so he avoids the majority play and always bets against the public. The professional will wager when two things present themselves together. First, his evaluation of the horses running must present a clear cut favorite determined by his handicapping criteria, and second, if the odds are 3 to 1 or better, he will then wager. The professional always has a game plan or strategy in any wager or bet that they engage in. The public never has a plan. The public is at the track gambling for entertainment and the professional is there to make money. These are two very different types of gambling.

The Stock Market Investor

The professional investor / speculator is fiercely independent. He can ride the tide when it pleases his portfolio strategy but he is willing to buck the trend and be a contrarian if necessary. He has invested time in learning how the markets and business cycles work. He is comfortable with research and data analysis. He is willing to admit when he is wrong, and can act on it. He will learn from and analyze his mistakes. He will have a game plan, an exit strategy, and the intestinal fortitude to see them through. He can control his emotions and walk the fine line between discipline and flexibility.

The Non Professionals

Here is a short list of non-professional gamblers and the games they play (pun intended.) These are completely random games requiring no skill, are for entertainment only, and cannot be lost on purpose. These games are played by people who can be heavily influenced by luck and superstition and their belief therein. Some believe they will pick the winning lottery numbers if they go to the churchyard cemetery at midnight, with a leather bag filled with 3 chicken bones, and swing it counter clockwise over their head while jumping up and down... These are the games a professional will not engage in, as he cannot gain an edge.

THE PLAYERS

Lottery
Slots
Bingo
Roulette
Keno
Craps
Coin flipping
Dice
Marriage (just kidding?)

Human Nature. Friend or Foe?

Plans, Emotions, and

Second Guessing.

Investing is contrary to basic human nature and it is of the utmost importance that you understand that fact. Please reread the last sentence. If I could carve that sentence in your forehead with a rusty nail I would. It is that important.

> *"Everybody has a plan until they*
> *get punched in the face."*
> *- Mike Tyson*

Tyson's quote is excellent, and makes a great point: every good boxer enters the ring with a plan that exploits his opponent's weaknesses and defends against his opponent's strengths. Then he gets hit in the face. So far, all the boxer knows about his plan is that he got *HIT* in the face. At

17

that moment, in his mind, the plan sucks! The plan is no longer any good. Does he consider his plan a failure or does he think luck has provided his opponent an opening? Does he stick with the plan or begin flailing wildly? All he really knows is **HE GOT HIT IN THE FACE!** And it **HURT!** Battle strategy says stick with the plan. However, many boxers have, on the fly, decided to go toe to toe in an all-out slug fest, much to the dismay of their managers. Changing horses in midstream is never recommended. Stick with the plan. This applies equally to investing. Stick with the plan.

You may want to stick to your investment strategies and you may think you are smart enough to do so, but, basic human nature will have you second guessing all of your sound financial decisions and seeing wisdom where none exists. Your brain is incredibly complex and predictable all at the same time. You should take a few minutes and get to know that 3 lb. mystery that lives between your ears.

You could have the best market timing, trading strategies, stock value analysis data, market indicators and bellwethers in place and YOU can still, metaphorically, get hit in the face. If you think, for one second, this will not have an immediate and dramatic effect on you, you would be wrong. Risk tolerance and loss aversion are very important concepts in relation to investing and ones that you need to be intimately familiar with. When you go to Las Vegas you play with chips. Want to know why? Because if it were actual money on the table your reactions would be different to losing. If you are betting small little plastic disks, who cares? We're having fun right? That's not money, those are little plastic chips. Let it ride! Aren't they cute? As long as it is not actual money on the table your reactions to losing will be different.

Here is an example from a study designed to measure loss aversion, a simple investment game: you start with $20 and you get to invest 1 dollar per round to play, or you can keep the dollar. If you invest / play, the experimenter takes your dollar and flips a coin. Heads you lose the dollar but, tails you win $2.50. When presented with this scenario, my response is let it ride all day long. I am going to lunch. I'll be back for my winnings. How long would you play? Based on the odds which are 50/50 which means that on average, half of the time you will lose $1 and half of the time you will win $2.50, logic says to play as long as they will let you. Right? However, if you think the average person would do that you would be wrong.

Something magical happens when a person actually touches that dollar bill. It becomes "theirs." It is somehow worth more. "The endowment effect" kicks in – the tendency for people to value an object more highly when they possess it than they would otherwise value the same object if they did not possess it. And they now have an emotional attachment to that dollar bill. Don't dismiss the emotional attachment! It can have major ramifications in your decision making process. Normal people who process emotions correctly will invest / play that game less than 60% of the time. People with lesions in their brains that do not experience emotions will play 83.7% of the time. And these emotionless investors, after losing a coin toss would invest 85.2% of the time. So in future, remember emotions and the painful memories of losing can really cloud your judgment and cause you to make irrational investment decisions.

Your 3 Pound Mystery

The brain is hard wired to seek out patterns. It is a survival instinct. If you recognize a pattern you may stop a bad scenario from happening a second time. Memories are hard coded to emotions, and the more unpleasant an emotion, the more vividly an experience is burned into your memory. In other words, you will always remember the things that created the most pain or discomfort more than you will remember the pleasant things that happen in your life. A child only needs to touch a hot stove once to realize that that is a bad idea. A cat that tries to sit on a hot stove, will not only no longer not sit on a hot stove, it will also not sit on a cold one. This pattern recognition could be life-saving. If you didn't recognize the pattern you may spend your life banging your head against the same wall making the same poor decisions day after day.

The brain, while trying to see patterns, may be fooled by randomness and identify a pattern where none exists and this is where your difficulty making investment decisions may come into play. As Kahneman and Tversky noted in their study on loss aversion, there are systematic aberrations in human behavior that are incompatible with rationality. Did you get that? It bears repeating. Systematic aberrations in human behavior that are incompatible with rationality! If we fail to realize how humans perceive risk we will make disastrous, irrational decisions and mismanage risk. Loss aversion is a powerful force behind your decision making and the pain you get from your losses is 2 times more potent than any good feelings you may get from your wins. Failing to recognize the power of loss aversion and perceived risk is not good in the long run for investment decisions.

The brain's desire for pattern recognition and the way you process loss aversion can have you selling winners and not only holding losers but purchasing more of your losers, doubling down, averaging down. These tendencies can also have you investing in securities with less risk and can result in lower returns. Your investments need to be tied to your own personal level of risk that you can accept and, more importantly, sleep with.

Experience Speaks Volumes

"There is nothing like losing all you have in the world for teaching you what not to do."
- Jesse Livermore

I always believed it was easier to learn from other's mistakes than suffer your own. I still believe that. I think you might too since you are reading this book. Financial lessons can be devastating to learn. If you went back in time you could ask Jessie Livermore, a self-made man and one of the greatest investors of all time, about devastating financial decisions. The man made, and lost, million dollar fortunes, repeatedly. He paid dearly for the financial lessons he learned. Ultimately he took his life after suffering yet another massive loss in the market which he readily explained was due to the fact that he ignored his own sound judgment and acted on advice from an acquaintance. This was in direct opposition to "the investment rules" Livermore had identified and successfully used routinely. On advice from someone else, he sold a winner and bought a loser. The perfect trifecta of bad investment decisions. Livermore was always an advocate of: knowing the current market trends, conducting your own research, formulating your own opinions, and most importantly, letting your winners run and ruthlessly cutting your losses.

"I can calculate the movement of stars, but not the madness of men."
- Sir Isaac Newton

Sir Isaac Newton, English physicist and mathematician, widely regarded as one of the top scientific minds of all time, was not immune from the lure of investment and speculation or the problems associated with poor investment decisions clouded by emotion and loss aversion. Having profited handsomely from the sale of his shares of the South Sea Company early in 1720, Newton could not stand by and watch the South Sea Company stock price continue to go through the roof. His friends were getting rich and he was out of the market and missing the boat. The meteoric rise of the stock could no longer be ignored by Newton and he re-entered the foray at just shy of the pinnacle of the bubble. He reinvested heavily with the share purchase price more than 3 times his original purchase price. We have all heard "what goes up must come down." Well, just as the South Sea Company had a meteoric rise in stock price, it also had the ensuing cataclysmic drop. Newton failed to cut his losses and rode that decline all the way to the bottom and his financial ruin.

Basic human nature is what it is, and has kept us all alive. Instinct and habit are hard to ignore. Emotions can overwhelm anyone. You are in good company. My advice: do your homework, have a plan, decide on an exit strategy and invest intelligently. Emotional speculation will be your undoing every time.

7 Winning Strategies

All the strategies presented here are simple and straight forward. You should not have to spend endless hours researching each company. Investment vehicles used, and the accounts they will work in, are listed in each strategy. Many of these strategies rely on mechanical and seasonal investment plans.

Remember, investing is NOT entertainment. You are not rolling the dice in Vegas. You are implementing and executing well thought out plans with structure and defined end points. Emotion should be controlled. The professional gambler's goal is to look for an advantage, take a calculated risk and make money using systematic and disciplined wagers, not to expose capital to undue, open ended risk. You would do well to treat investing like a game with a set of rules to follow and defined end points. If you do so you will be less likely to incur losses due to psychological factors.

Speculation can be defined as thinking and then acting, whereas, acting and then thinking defines betting (trying to be right) or gambling (looking for excitement). Betting or gambling is what you engage in at the tables in Vegas and those activities have defined end points. The hand is over, the wheel has spun, the dice stopped rolling and your losses are curtailed automatically. Not so in the market. If you try to apply emotional decisions, gut feelings, betting or gambling strategies to market speculation which is an open ended ongoing risk activity, where the fun doesn't stop, you could get more excitement than you bargained for.

Be a smart speculator. Have a goal. Have a plan. Have an exit strategy in place. Keep your emotions out of your decision making process and stick to your plan.

RECAP: Before we go on to the strategies, unless otherwise stated, the investment vehicle we will be using is the S&P 500 represented in your 401k as the large cap index fund and available in your self-directed IRA as the Exchange Traded Fund (ETF) with the ticker symbol SPY.

Please be aware that when I reference SPY and SPX they are both the same except that SPY is the Exchange Traded Fund you will be purchasing in your accounts and SPX is the ticker symbol for the S&P 500.

Turn of the Month

Turn of the Month is a very interesting, low risk, easy investment strategy that limits your exposure to market volatility while exposing you to the best trading days of the month.

This strategy will work in both your 401k and your IRA. The ETF to use will be SPY in the IRA, and in your 401k you will make your best effort to pick a fund that tracks to the S&P 500. Because of trading restrictions in the 401k (such as a 30 day limit) you may have to choose two funds and alternate between them. A good choice would be a large cap index fund and a mid-cap index fund.

Turn of the Month will have you invested for 4 days of the month, total: the last trading day and the first 3 trading days of the month. Historically these 4 days provide the most gains and this strategy limits your exposure to risk and market volatility by having you out of the market the rest of the month. According to multiple studies, the remaining 16 days provide no reward to the investor for bearing market risk.

If you can garner the same gain in a smaller time frame you are far better off. You are exposed to less market volatility. I would rather be invested for one fifth of the time and reap the benefit of the most profitable trading days. I can use the rest of the month to sit in cash and gain risk free interest or explore some other beneficial play that may be available.

Lakonishok and Smidt (1988) did a study on the Dow Jones Industrial Average (DJIA,) between 1897 – 1986, which identified a pattern of trading days where unusually high returns were earned. They described this pattern as "The Turn of the Month Effect."

Wei Xu and John McConnell of Purdue University published a paper in July of 2006 on Equity Returns at the Turn of the Month which further studied the seasonal anomaly. They analyzed the DJIA between 1987 - 2005 (and 1897 - 2005). Their results confirm that cumulatively over the time period of 1897-2005 all of the positive returns to the DJIA occurred during the Turn of the Month interval.

The following chart from the Wu and McConnell paper clearly shows their results.

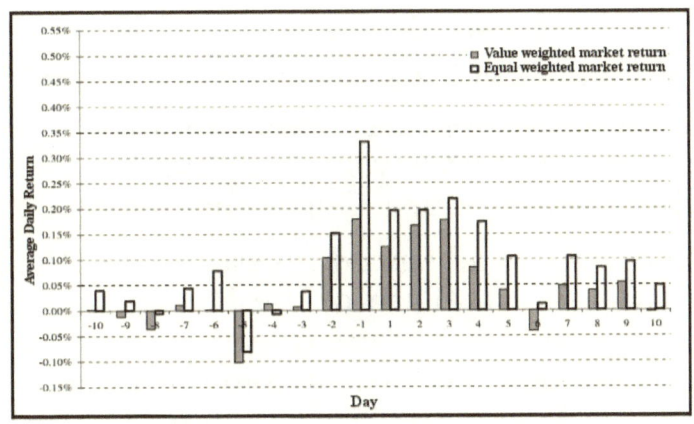

Average daily value-weighted and equal-weighted market returns for the last 10 trading days and the first 10 trading days of the month, 1926-2005. You can access a larger image of this graph and other resources by visiting the website.

http://www.reluctantbull.com/gamblers-guide

For the advanced investor, this strategy can also be utilized with a 5 or even a 7 day window. Example, the last 2 trading days of the month and the first 3 trading days of the month or the last 3 trading days of the month and the first 4 trading days of the month. Money can flood the market in this window of time as investors will use available cash for last minute, month end purchases, brokers will try to generate month end commissions by using any extra client cash on hand, and fund managers will window dress investments by manipulating their returns to shore up their month end reports. Automated monthly contributions to 401ks and IRAs hit accounts in this window of time too, generating a glut of positive performance in the markets.

In addition, you may want to utilize an equal weighted ETF (SPX is value weighted) as they can provide a better return. Guggenheim offers RSP.

Also, for the advanced investor, and ONLY in your IRAs for the Turn of the Month strategy, if you are up on your trade (meaning that you are in profit on this investment) and the strategy says sell, you may want to place a tight trailing stop on your trade, in case it continues its upward path. This way, you can continue to hold the stock as it rises even beyond the general sell time until the market turns in order to maximize profits. (A Trailing Stop: The trailing stop is an exit point strategy for your trade. The purpose of the trailing stop order is to protect, or lock in, your profits on a trade. You set up a trailing stop in advance so that you do not have to personally watch the stock every minute of the day. It is a kind of automated sell trigger that says to sell this stock if the stock price falls by either a preset percentage or dollar amount.)

Sell in May and Go Away. Really?

"Sell in May and Go Away" is based on the historical trend that the market, on average, goes up during the period of time between November 1st and May 1st. Historically, 80% of the gains are made in this window of time. From May 1st until November 1st there can still be gains made but to a much smaller extent of approximately 20%. While these numbers are not set in stone, an approximate 80% - 20% relationship exists.

If you understand what is going on at different times of the year you can understand why this market timing strategy should work and previously has proven a winning strategy. During that golden sweet spot, between November 1st and May 1st you have many economic factors coming into play.

Some examples of the economic factors that make the "Sell in May and Go Away" strategy work are as follows: Consumer spending is greatest during this period of time. Purchases for unnecessary items rise. Think Christmas and the holidays. The lion's share of retail profits are made during the holidays. Cruises and family vacations are often booked and paid for in this time frame. Money floods the market as year-end bonuses are paid, 401k contributions are deposited in the employee's accounts and savvy investors fund their retirement accounts.

Executive compensation (typically paid in March) and corporate bonuses for management are paid in this window as well and these can be some astronomical amounts. Executive compensation, on average for the top 500 companies in America, is approximately 10.5 million. That amount of money has to go somewhere and it will have an effect on the markets.

Expected tax refunds also contribute to the glut of money flooding the markets at this time too. As an example, early in the year car dealers will do a customer's taxes for free as soon as the W-2s start arriving. The end game being that the consumer walks in with his tax records and leaves the dealership with a car. Many companies try and make it as easy as possible to separate the consumer from their tax refund. Rest assured that this technique is not going unnoticed by other retailers.

Sell in May and Go Away as a strategy can be utilized in 3 different ways or variations. Some versions produce markedly larger returns. This, of course, depends on how active you would like to be with your investments and how closely you plan on watching and adjusting your investments.

You need to decide on the level of risk you are willing to take and on the amount of time you have to personally and actively manage your portfolio.

All versions of this strategy will have you fully invested in the broad market between November 1st and May 1st. That is the golden period of time where 7.8% of the yearly 9.6% gains, on average, are made in the market. All these strategies have to do with the question "What do you do with your investments during the period between May 1st and November 1st when the market typically only returns 1.8% on average?" The third variation can only be used in a self-directed IRA as your 401k will more than likely not have fund options that will work with this strategy and version 3 will have you investing in different exchange traded funds from the first 2 versions.

Version 1 of Sell in May and Go Away

The first version is just what it states, Sell in May and Go Away. This variation is for use within your retirement account. If you have a 401k and have to pick from the funds they offer you, you would be using the investment option available to you that best tracks to the S&P 500. If your 401k choices do not include a large cap index fund that tracks the S&P 500, an equal split between a large cap growth fund and a large cap value fund will reasonably mimic an S&P 500 index fund.

If you are instituting this plan in your self-directed IRA then you would be invested in the ETF with the ticker symbol SPY (the exchange traded fund SPY uses the S&P 500 as an index and that fund will own shares in the companies that are listed in the index). You could also use a managed mutual fund but the fees would be greater and if you are really only trying to buy the broad market then the S&P 500 is the best option out there and the fees are considerably less with the ETF SPY than with a managed mutual fund. The managed mutual fund is redundant in this case as all that the fund managers would be buying in their fund would be the same S&P 500 companies listed in the index that you would buy yourself as an ETF.

This strategy has you selling your investments come May 1st every year and holding cash or going into a risk free interest bearing vehicle for the next 6 months, something like a CD or money market account.

The problem with this version, and why I do not recommend it, is that you would do better with a buy and hold strategy than this strategy since gains are still made within the window between May 1st and November 1st. Plain old buy and hold would provide a better return.

Version 2 of Sell in May and Go Away

The second version of Sell in May and Go Away is more creative and will require more of your time but will also hopefully keep you invested when returns are to be had and out when the market is declining. Version 2 is still the same as version 1 for the period between November 1st and May 1st when you will be fully invested in the broad market (S&P 500) using either your 401k's plan offering or you will be using the ETF SPY in the IRA.

During the period between May 1st and November 1st we will use the 200 day moving average for SPY as a filter to determine whether or not we should be in or out of the market.

The 200 day moving average is an indicator which investors use to analyze price trends. It is simply a security's average closing price over the last 200 days. The 200 day moving average chart can be easily generated using a free charting service on the Internet. You can access a 200 day moving average chart for SPX at Bigcharts.com or use one of the many other charting services. It would be in your best interest to learn how to use these free tools.

Ideally, you will want to evaluate your position weekly. If the share price of SPY is above the 200 day moving average for SPY, then the strategy says that you should be invested in the market. In other words, you should purchase SPY or stay in the market if you are already invested. When the share price for SPY falls below the 200 day moving average for SPY, then the strategy says that you would want to be out of the market and you would sell your position in SPY. You will, of course, only reenter the market during the period between May 1st and November 1st, when the share price for SPY again goes above the 200 day moving average. You would then use your proceeds to buy back in. Otherwise, you would stay out until November 1st when the strategy has you buying back in.

When utilizing this plan in your 401k you might come up against a 30 day limit for trading in a specific fund, a transfer restriction as an example. Some 401k plans prohibit you from reentering an investment option for 30 days after you exit that same investment option. If the strategy calls for you to reenter the market in that restricted time frame, make your best attempt to pick investment options that mimic the S&P 500 such as the growth / value split mentioned in Version 1 of Sell in May and Go Away listed above. A mid cap index fund would also make an acceptable proxy.

Version 3 of Sell in May and Go Away

The third version of Sell in May and Go Away has you swapping Consumer Staples and Consumer Discretionary funds every 6 months.

To execute this strategy you will purchase the exchange traded fund XLY (representing consumer discretionary sector) October 28th and sell it April 27th. You will then use the proceeds to purchase the exchange traded fund XLP (representing consumer staples sector) April 28th

and sell it October 27th. Lather, rinse and repeat. The dates referenced here are approximate depending on how the trading days fall in the calendar month. Try and catch the last 3 trading days of October when buying XLY (consumer discretionary sector) for the November through May period and sell your position so that you can catch the last 3 trading days of April when you switch to XLP (consumer staples sector) for the May through November period.

You will be invested in the discretionary sector during the winter and spring months as this is the time that discretionary dollars are flowing into the market and stock prices typically rise. You will be invested in consumer staples during the summer and early fall when there is less volatility and the consumer staples sector typically performs better.

Remember, for any plan to work you need to stick to your strategy. If you go with your own intuition you will be out of the market when you need to be in and vice versa. The average investor is ruled by emotions. Do not let your emotions cloud your investment decisions. Decide on a plan and stick with it. Check out the table and chart to see the long term results of this strategy. The sample shown is not as long as I would have liked but Exchange traded funds are a relatively new investment vehicle.

Please note that this strategy will require a self-directed IRA. Most 401ks will not provide options necessary to execute this strategy.

Below is a table and a chart displaying the results of this strategy from May of 2001 to November of 2014. As compared to a buy and hold strategy using SPX (representing the S&P 500 broad market) the results are very dramatic and there appears to be a clear winner. These numbers represent simple percentage gains and do not include compounding interest which will generally affect your returns in a positive way. You can access pdf files of these resources by visiting the website.

http://www.reluctantbull.com/gamblers-guide

Consumer Discretionary & Staples ETF Swap Strategy			
Time Frame*		ETF	% Gain
5/1/2001	11/1/2001	staples xlp	0
11/1/2001	5/1/2002	disc xly	19.00
5/1/2002	11/1/2002	staples xlp	-13
11/1/2002	5/1/2003	disc xly	3.00
5/1/2003	11/1/2003	staples xlp	11
11/1/2003	5/1/2004	disc xly	3.75
5/1/2004	11/1/2004	staples xlp	-6.5
11/1/2004	5/1/2005	disc xly	-5.00
5/1/2005	11/1/2005	staples xlp	0.5
11/1/2005	5/1/2006	disc xly	5.00
5/1/2006	11/1/2006	staples xlp	7.8
11/1/2006	5/1/2007	disc xly	5.75
5/1/2007	11/1/2007	staples xlp	2
11/1/2007	5/1/2008	disc xly	-7.00
5/1/2008	11/1/2008	staples xlp	-14
11/1/2008	5/1/2009	disc xly	4.00
5/1/2009	11/1/2009	staples xlp	17.5
11/1/2009	5/1/2010	disc xly	29.00
5/1/2010	11/1/2010	staples xlp	3
11/1/2010	5/1/2011	disc xly	15.00
5/1/2011	11/1/2011	staples xlp	-3.5
11/1/2011	5/1/2012	disc xly	20.00
5/1/2012	11/1/2012	staples xlp	3.5
11/1/2012	5/1/2013	disc xly	16.50
5/1/2013	11/1/2013	staples xlp	4
11/1/2013	5/1/2014	disc xly	1.00
5/1/2014	11/1/2014	staples xlp	5.5
		Total Return	127.8
* If buy date weekend or holiday use next trading date			

You can access a pdf of this table online by visiting the website.

http://www.reluctantbull.com/gamblers-guide

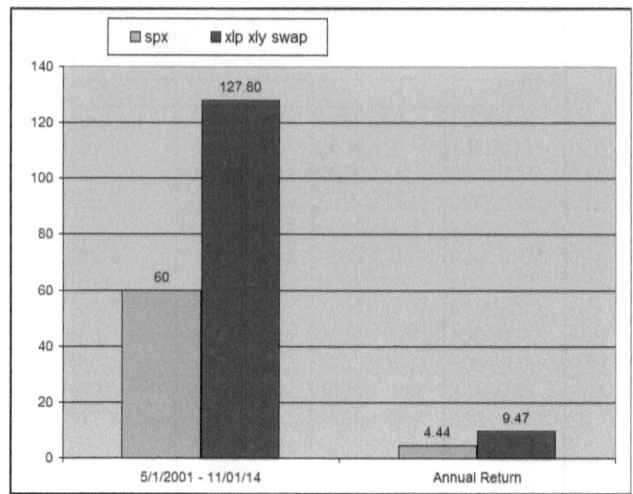

Comparison percentage gains for SPX buy and hold versus XLP, XLY swap strategies from 5/01/2001 - 11/01/2014 and average annual returns.

You can access a pdf of this graph online by visiting the website.

http://www.reluctantbull.com/gamblers-guide

Dogs of the DOW 2.0

Dogs of the DOW is a yearly strategy that calls for an investor, at year end, to buy the 10 highest yielding stocks listed on the Dow Jones Industrial Average (DJIA). The DJIA is a price weighted index comprised of 30 of the most widely traded large cap companies. These are the big blue chip stocks of the market. The 10 highest yielding stocks have a higher yield as their share price has been beaten down and they may be out of favor with investors. Hence the name, Dogs of the Dow.

With this strategy, at the end of every year you rebalance your portfolio. You take the total value of the portfolio, add any additional contributions, and you distribute the balance evenly between the 10 new dogs for the year. You sell any companies that are no longer on the list, and you may have to sell a few shares of one or two companies so that you end up with the total value of your portfolio divided evenly between the 10 current dogs.

You could further increase your returns by executing something called the Mini Dogs of the

Dow. Utilizing this strategy you buy only 5 stocks with the lowest share price from the Dogs of the Dow list. This gives you a greater possibility of share price appreciation at the cost of diversification because you are investing in fewer companies.

Below is a chart comparing the strategies of investing in the DJIA, the Dogs of the Dow and the Mini Dogs for the past 20 years. You can access a larger version of this chart by visiting the website.

http://www.reluctantbull.com/gamblers-guide

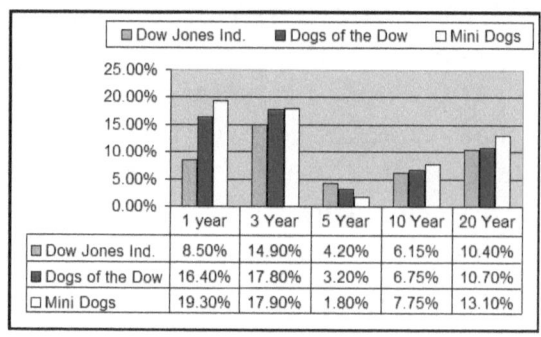

	1 year	3 Year	5 Year	10 Year	20 Year
▥ Dow Jones Ind.	8.50%	14.90%	4.20%	6.15%	10.40%
■ Dogs of the Dow	16.40%	17.80%	3.20%	6.75%	10.70%
☐ Mini Dogs	19.30%	17.90%	1.80%	7.75%	13.10%

Another variation you could use would be the Dogs of the S&P 100. For this strategy, start with the top 100 companies listed in the S&P 500. Now take only the top 10 yielding companies from this list. The Dogs of the S&P 100 has a larger sample (100 companies versus 30 on the Dow) so it provides a broader segment and allows for the possibility of deeper diversification from which to select your investments. You rebalance this portfolio annually, the same as in the previous version.

Since 1957, the Dogs of the Dow have returned 12.6% per year and the Dogs of the S&P returned an outstanding 14.10% per year. Compounded over the years, the Dogs of the S&P's greater rate of return of 1.5% could make a big difference to your bottom line.

Laddered Splits

Stock splits, the theory behind companies using them, and their results, have people in 2 different camps.

One group will adamantly tell you that a stock split is a non-event, a simple accounting function with no relationship to stock performance or share price. A simple 2 for 1 split is where you end up with twice as many shares at half the price. All things remain equal. This camp will say you are foolish to believe otherwise in regards to stock splits and consequent positive share price performance.

The second group will tell you that Corporate America will use stock splits as a marketing strategy to engender investor goodwill. Some companies believe their stock is more attractive to small investors at certain price points. Investors tend to view stock splits as an indication of strong growth potential going forward. Executives will have a target range for their stock share price, and if the stock trades well above that range, and they believe that the higher price is not temporary, a split is likely to occur to bring stock share price back to the target range. This group believes splits have a positive impact on share price and performance especially in the short term.

Numerous studies support the second group's thinking. In 1996, a study by David Ikenberry of Rice University analyzed 2 for 1 splits between 1975 and 1990. He compared his data to a control group of similar sized and similar sector companies that had not split. Results were dramatic and statistically significant. His study revealed that companies which had done 2 for 1 splits had an 8% performance increase better than the control group for the first year and 16% better performance after 3 years.

Subsequent studies by Ikenberry and others confirm the results that demonstrate outstanding, abnormal returns and positive price reactions from stock splits.

Laddered splits is a simple strategy that calls for you to purchase independent stocks in your IRA that have recently undergone a stock split and hold those investments for 12 to 36 months. That is the time frame the studies indicate that there are outstanding, abnormal returns to be had. Cycle your investments out when they have run the course and replace with new, recently split stocks. You only need to check your portfolio as often as you intend to hold the securities: for example 12, 24 or 36 months. If you have many split stocks available to choose from you could do this on a 12 month cycle and reap the largest gains as they typically happen in the first year after the split occurs. If you don't find a good candidate to switch to you could hold for longer than 12 months while searching for another stock that has split. Just track how long you have owned a stock after it has split. Your best returns will be in the following 3 years post stock split.

There are additional criteria you should use to determine which stocks to purchase for this strategy. Just because a stock has split does not mean that it is a good candidate to purchase. Two criteria that you should use are price/earnings ratio and dividend yield. Post split stocks that are trading with a low price/earnings ratio, preferably under 20, and / or stocks that pay a dividend will perform best. Both of these criteria will hopefully be indicative of a quality company that is splitting for positive reasons.

Also make sure that your portfolio is diversified. Do not expose yourself to undue risk by having all of your investments in one sector. For example, instead of having all utilities stocks you would want to have some drug, some industrial and some electronics stocks in order to insulate your portfolio from an unanticipated problem with your favorite stock sector (the sectors listed here are not a recommendation just used as an example only.)

Presidential Election Cycle

Investment decisions can be based on repetitive historic market patterns. The 4 year presidential election cycle represents one of the best patterns.

Minimal growth is experienced in the first two years of the 4 year presidential election cycle. The newly elected president may institute policies that the market perceives as unfavorable. His agenda in the first 2 years may be highly unpopular. Whereas, in the last 2 years, the president may be trying to get reelected and start doing things to facilitate his reelection. The market has generally responded well to the second half of the presidential cycle.

There is a very old and simple investment strategy based on the presidential election cycle: in the first 2 years you go to cash and the last 2 years (approximately) you go to stocks. If you had implemented this strategy in your retirement accounts historically you would have done spectacularly well.

In the first 2 years which are historically rather flat, you would be in cash (CDs,

Treasuries...) and out of the markets. While you are out of the market you will be safe from market volatility, enjoying an interest based, virtually risk free, return. There is still money to be made in the first 2 years of the presidential cycle, but, without the wind at your back from the president's administration instituting market friendly policies significant returns may be harder to come by in this period of time.

It is easier to make money when the US government has got your back and is clearing a path to prosperity, as opposed to standing in your way, throwing up road blocks. As with one of our other strategies, "Don't fight the Central Banks," the same advice applies: don't buck the trend, swim with the current.

When the new president is sworn in, in early January, go to cash. One year and 10 months after the inauguration, (November 1st) switch from cash to stocks until the next inauguration day two years and 2 months later. Rinse and repeat. In other words, the first 2 years (really 22 months) of the presidential cycle you would be in cash and the last 2 years (really 26 months) you would be fully invested in the market using SPY in your IRA or an S&P 500 index fund in your 401k.

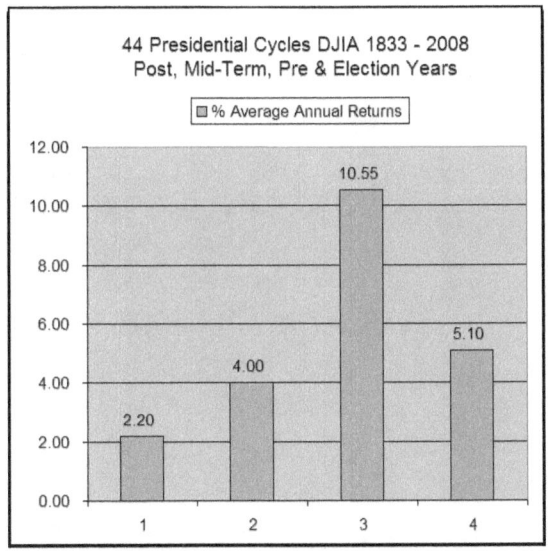

You can access a larger image of this chart online by visiting the website.

http://www.reluctantbull.com/gamblers-guide.

PRESIDENTIAL ELECTION CYCLE

			44 Presidential Cycles DJIA 1833 - 2008			
Year Elected	President	Party	Post Election	Mid-Term	Pre-Election	Election Year
1832	Jackson	D	(0.90)	13.00	3.10	(11.70)
1836	Van Buren	D	(11.50)	1.60	(12.30)	5.50
1840	W. H. Harrison	W	(13.30)	(18.10)	45.00	15.50
1844	Polk	D	8.10	(14.50)	1.20	(3.60)
1848	Taylor	W	0.00	18.70	(3.20)	19.60
1852	Pierce	D	(12.70)	(30.20)	1.50	4.40
1856	Buchanan	D	(31.00)	14.30	(10.70)	14.00
1860	Lincoln	R	(1.80)	55.40	38.00	6.40
1862	Lincoln	R	(8.50)	3.60	1.60	10.80
1868	Grant	R	1.70	5.60	7.30	6.80
1872	Grant	R	(12.70)	2.80	(4.10)	(17.90)
1876	Hayes	R	(9.40)	6.10	43.00	18.70
1880	Garfield	R	3.00	(2.90)	(8.50)	(18.80)
1884	Cleveland	D	20.10	12.40	(8.40)	4.80
1888	B. Harrison	R	5.50	(14.10)	17.60	(6.60)
1892	Cleveland	D	(24.60)	(0.60)	2.30	(1.70)
1896	McKinley	R	21.30	22.50	9.20	7.00
1900	McKinley	R	(8.70)	(0.40)	(23.60)	41.70
1904	T Roosevelt	R	38.20	(1.90)	(37.70)	16.60
1908	Taft	R	15.00	(17.90)	0.40	7.60
1912	Wilson	D	(10.30)	(5.40)	81.70	(4.20)
1916	Wilson	D	(21.70)	10.50	30.50	(32.90)
1920	Herding	R	12.10	21.70	(3.30)	26.20
1924	Coolidge	R	30.00	0.30	28.80	48.20
1928	Hoover	R	(17.20)	(33.80)	(52.70)	(23.10)
1932	F. Roosevelt	D	66.70	4.10	38.50	24.80
1936	F. Roosevelt	D	(32.80)	28.10	(2.90)	(12.70)
1940	F. Roosevelt	D	(15.40)	7.60	13.80	12.10

1944	F Roosevelt	D	26.60	(8.10)	2.20	(2.10)
1948	Truman	D	12.90	17.60	14.40	8.40
1952	Eisenhower	R	(3.80)	44.00	20.80	2.30
1956	Eisenhower	R	(12.80)	34.00	16.40	(9.30)
1960	Kennedy	D	18.70	(10.80)	17.00	14.60
1964	Johnson	D	10.90	(18.90)	15.20	4.30
1968	Nixon	R	(15.20)	4.80	6.10	14.60
1972	Nixon	R	(16.60)	(27.60)	38.32	17.86
1976	Carter	D	(17.27)	(3.15)	4.19	14.93
1980	Reagan	R	(9.23)	19.61	20.27	(3.74)
1984	Reagan	R	57.66	22.58	2.26	11.85
1988	G. H. W. Bush	R	26.96	(4.34)	20.32	4.17
1992	Clinton	D	13.72	2.14	33.45	26.01
1996	Clinton	D	22.64	16.10	25.22	(6.18)
2000	G. W. Bush	R	(7.10)	(16.76)	25.32	3.15
2004	G. W. Bush	R	(0.61)	16.29	6.43	(33.84)
	% Total Gain		96.67	175.97	463.98	224.51
	% Average Years Returns		**2.20**	**4.00**	**10.55**	**5.10**
	# of Years with Positive Returns		20	26	33	29
	# of Years with Negative Returns		24	18	11	15
	% of Years with Positive Returns		45	59	75	66
	% of Years with Negative Returns		55	41	25	34

You can access a pdf of this data online, by visiting the website.

http://www.reluctantbull.com/gamblers-guide

Don't Fight the Central Banks

One of the first things you learn as a broker is "don't fight the Fed." This is one of the oldest rules in investing. Since we live in a global economy, the rule should really be "Don't Fight the Central Banks." Axioms like "swim with the current" or "don't buck the trend" explain the mentality behind this rule. When the central banks are actively trying to stimulate the economy money will find a way into the markets. Since the downturn in 2008 many investors were completely surprised by, and missed the boat, in regards to the post 2009 rally in the markets.

The Federal Reserve System, more commonly known as The Fed, is the central bank for the United States. The Federal Reserve Act, signed into law by Woodrow Wilson December 23rd, 1913, created The Federal Reserve. The Fed has four areas of responsibilities:

1. Create monetary policy to influence money and credit conditions in the economy in pursuit of full employment and stable prices.

2. Supervise and regulate the banks and other financial institutions ensuring the safety and soundness of the nation's banking and financial systems and to protect consumer credit rights.

3. Maintain stability and contain systemic risk in the financial markets.

4. Provide financial services to the US government, US financial institutions, foreign official institutions and the Fed plays a major role in operating and overseeing the nation's payment systems.

Quantitative easing, "QE" for short, is a monetary stimulus policy instituted by Ben Bernanke, the chairman of the Federal Reserve. The first round of QE started in November 2008. The intent was to steer the world's largest economy through the depths of the financial crisis, away from a fiscal cliff and a true depression. The Fed started by unveiling an $800 billion plan to bolster lending institutions and the housing markets. In March of 2009 the Fed announced plans to buy $300 billion in long term treasury bonds. This was followed in November of 2010 by the Fed pledging to buy $600 billion in long term treasury bonds. The Fed went through numerous rounds of QE through 2014. In an effort at further stimulus the Fed vows to keep interest rates low for the foreseeable future as well. The last statement is true as of the time of this writing early 2015.

Bernanke had studied the Great Depression and was certain that ineffective monetary policy was the reason for the protracted depression. He felt that the monetary policy employed during the depression was not of significant quantity or of sufficient duration to be effective. His policy of easy, available money, and low interest rates, and his dedication to it earned him the nickname "Helicopter Ben." It was said that he was so devoted to the success of his policy that, if needed, he would fly over the country and drop money out of the sky. He was committed to keeping the US from falling into a protracted depression.

When the central banks are employing these types of policies and stimulating the economy with such vast amounts of money you would do well to take note and go along for the ride. This money will find a way to the markets. Hence the post 2009 rally in the markets

"Mini Annuities"

Annuities always entice people with their claims of unlimited payouts. The benefit of an annuity is that it is able to provide a lifetime steady stream of income. They do have a place in some people's portfolios. But to me, if something sounds too good to be true, it usually is.

One of the problems with annuities is that they are not indexed to inflation. You can buy one that is indexed to inflation but you will get a lower payout. You can also purchase an annuity with a spousal benefit but that will further reduce your payout.

The biggest problem with an annuity, and a fact that the sales person will not dwell on, is that **the investor's original money is gone forever**. That fact is insurmountable in regards to your investment and the return on your investment. Your returns are based on a dollar value of initial purchase but ALL your capital is GONE. Never to be seen again by you. How many years will the insurance company simply be giving you back your own money?

If you analyze the results that an annuity provides for your period of investment, the numbers are not good. By the way, we all have already funded an annuity, it is called Social Security. Social Security and the following strategy are both adjusted for inflation.

The idea of an annuity, however, is very attractive. Who wouldn't want a guaranteed return, in good times and bad, for life? Well I suggest building your own "annuities" with a concept I call "Mini Annuities."

My Mini Annuities are individual stocks you purchase for the long term. What matters is what kind of stocks you chose. You need solid, stable companies that provide a steady stream of income in the form of a dividend. I like to use the Dividend Aristocrats list for my Mini Annuities. This list is made up of companies whose mission statements include routinely returning a portion of the profits to the shareholder via dividends. The Aristocrat list is comprised of companies that have raised their dividends for 25 years or more.

The strategy calls for you to purchase companies from the Dividend Aristocrat list and hold them for the long term. Your portfolio would only have to be looked at yearly. As an example, you would purchase a dozen different stocks from diversified sectors: energy, staples, high tech, etc. You check the Dividend Aristocrats list yearly and if your stock is still on the list you do nothing. If your stock fell off the Dividend

Aristocrat list you would sell and purchase another stock from the list.

The best thing about this strategy is that you keep your capital. With this strategy your age will come into play on how you initially institute the strategy. You don't need to care so much about share price if you are a young person with lots of time on your side for the miracle of compounding growth to occur. You are purchasing an income stream for the long term without having to surrender or relinquish your capital as you would if you bought a traditional annuity. Your intention with these stock purchases is to hold these stocks for the remainder of your life. Let your heirs worry about share price. This is your life savings and you want it to work for you but also let you sleep comfortably at night. If you are nearing retirement, you would want to use this strategy only during a market downturn as you need a decent initial yield as time is no longer on your side. See our example below in the "for the advanced investor" section.

What you do with the dividends will depend on whether you need to save now or you need income as you are at retirement age. As a young person, the ideal strategy would be to reinvest the dividends back into your portfolio. In the interest of diversification, I would suggest using the dividends to establish a position in a different Dividend Aristocrat and continue to further diversify until you have a well balanced mix of stocks in your portfolio from several different market sectors, example: tech, energy, health care, financial, utilities, etc. As a retiree you will be counting on the dividends as income.

When the subject of retirement comes up many of the experts will quote you an astronomical bulk number that you will need to finance your retirement. With a strategy like this all you have to figure out is how much your monthly income needs will be. Between your estimated Social Security and your dividend income you will have a good idea of what your monthly income will be. You are concerned with a monthly income instead of some mythical number needed to retire.

Any time you face a job change, job transfer, job loss, or new career, you would be well served to take the payout from your former employer's retirement account and roll it into a self-directed IRA and institute the Mini Annuities strategy. When your working career is over you will have a substantial, solid, retirement portfolio.

How else can you use the Mini Annuities strategy? How about using it to fund your child / grandchild/ren's retirement?

Many people get upset when they hear or read about "golden parachutes" that are enjoyed by the elite of Corporate America's top management. Please note, I am personally not offended by a business strategy that is designed to attract, keep and reward the top performing as well as the best and brightest business leaders in Corporate America and which results in keeping their respective businesses profitable. However, not many everyday people will ever have the opportunity to work in a job with that kind of Cadillac benefit. Nevertheless, if you are a parent or grandparent with some disposable cash and the desire to help set your child / grandchild/ren up for life, you could give, "gift them" their own golden parachute.

What do I mean? Check out a compounding interest calculator.

By funding your child / grandchild's IRA for just 6 years you could seed the start of a golden parachute which will significantly grow over time through the power of compound interest compliments of mom and dad or grandma and grandpa.

Take the following example for a home grown golden parachute. Assuming that your child / grandchild has a taxable income, you could chose to fund your child / grandchild's IRA. Use the Mini Annuities strategy to pick stocks from the Dividend Aristocrats list. With this strategy you could be giving them a phenomenal retirement. As of this writing in early 2015, you can currently gift up to $5,500 into a retirement account as long as the recipient, in this case your child / grandchild, actually has a taxable income of $5,500 or more for each gift year. Next, assume that from the time that your child / grandchild is 16 years old and for the next 6 years, which would be during the last 2 years of high school and for the first 4 years of college, if you funded his/her IRA with only $5,500 each year for 6 years, that would amount to $33,000 in direct contributions from you. However, even if your child / grandchild never put another penny in the account but left it alone to grow harnessing the incredible effect of compound interest and they earned an average return of 8% per year for 50 years, they would have an amazing $1,547,753.21 at retirement. A pretty good sized golden parachute!

I don't know about you but that would be a tremendous legacy from you. Most people leave a lump sum to their heirs when they die. Your heirs will use the inheritance for who knows what; buy a car, take a vacation, purchase a bigger house, pay off a bill... Think outside the box and set your heirs up early to be independently wealthy in their retirement years. Trust me; they will remember you very fondly. Also, make sure that they understand what that account is for and **NOT** to touch it until retirement age. Teach them about compounding interest.

For comparison purposes a general example between two different investors may help you see the point. A return rate of 10% is used for example only; your returns will likely be different. No one can predict what your returns will or will not be.

Thrifty Trish, starting at age 18, saves 2 thousand dollars a year for the first 10 years and then stops contributing (total contribution

$20,000.) At age 65 (assuming a 10% compounded return) she will have 1.3 million.

Procrastinating Pete, on the other hand, waited 10 years until he was age 28 to begin annual contributions of 2 thousand per year. Despite continuing his annual contribution of 2 thousand for the next 37 years (total contribution $76,000) at age 65 (assuming the same 10% compounded return) he will have amassed only 800 thousand dollars, trailing Thrifty Trish by over a half a million dollars.

Truly, the early bird does get the worm. Start those kids planning their retirement with their first paycheck. Even if you let them spend their paycheck take the long view and fund their retirement account for them.

The lesson here is illustrated wonderfully by the following quote.

"The most powerful force in the universe is compound interest."
- Albert Einstein

The best gift you could give your child, or grandchild, is teaching them to think, evaluate, and decide for themselves. Teach them good financial planning skills. Teach them what this kind of gift could mean to them. We are all subject to the life choices that we make and our financial decisions are a significant part of those choices. Every one of those choices will have consequences. We need to teach our children about consequences and their long term effects. Give them the gift of knowledge, so that they make good decisions. Share your wisdom. I only wish someone had told me this and made sure that I understood the information at a young age.

For the advanced investor, this strategy would work best if instituted in a market down turn. The lower your initial share price the better your long term yield will be.

Take for example 3M (ticker:MMM) in early 2009, the share price had fallen to $43 with a quarterly dividend of $0.51 per share and a yield of nearly 5%.

Fast forward to early 2015. With 6 years of dividend increases, the quarterly dividend is now $1.02 per share and your initial investment would now yield over 9%.

Therefore, if in 2009 you had seen that 3M had fallen drastically yet you were confident in the basic viability of the company and it remained on the Dividend Aristocrat list, then buying 3M in a down economy with the intent to hold for the long term would have been a great example of a stock to use in the Mini Annuity strategy.

The Finish Line

Price is what you pay. Value is what you get. Buying great companies (that could be run by idiots at some point and still profit), at discount prices, should be every investor's dream.

"Imitation is the sincerest form of flattery."
- Charles Caleb Colton

You could expand your knowledge of investing profitably by learning from the best investors. Here is a short list, in no particular order, with 7 of the greatest investors ever. This list is not complete by any means, but represents a good starting point for your further financial education. If you are reading the digital version of this book, for your convenience, I have made the titles clickable links to Amazon. Links to these resources can also be found on my website.

http://www.reluctantbull.com/gamblers-guide

ABOUT THE AUTHOR

Warren Buffet - Berkshire Hathaway Letters to Shareholders

Benjamin Graham - The Intelligent Investor: The Definitive Book on Value Investing. A Book of Practical Counsel (Revised Edition)

Jesse Livermore - Reminiscences of a Stock Operator

Philip Fisher - Common Stocks and Uncommon Profits and Other Writings

John Templeton - Templeton's Way with Money: Strategies and Philosophy of a Legendary Investor

Peter Lynch - One Up On Wall Street: How To Use What You Already Know To Make Money In The Market

David Dreman - Contrarian Investment Strategies: The Psychological Edge

"Men fear thought as they fear nothing else on earth - more than ruin - more even than death... Thought is subversive and revolutionary, destructive and terrible, thought is merciless to privilege, established institutions, and comfortable habit. Thought looks into the pit of hell and is not afraid. Thought is great and swift and free, the light of the world, and the chief glory of man."
- Bertrand Russell

Russell's quote is one of my favorites. The quote exemplifies the main theory behind this book. Think for yourself. Good luck.

Wishing you spectacular successes in your retirement planning.

You can visit my website Reluctantbull.com and sign up for free strategy updates and recommendations too. This link will let you sign up for the updates.

http://bit.ly/reluctantbull.

Thanks for taking the time to read the book. I hope you found it beneficial. If you don't mind, I would like to ask one favor of you: if this book

ABOUT THE AUTHOR

has helped you in any way, I would be grateful if you could share those thoughts in the form of a review on my book's page at Amazon.com, bn.com, kobo.com, apple.com or wherever you purchased my book. I appreciate the feedback.

~ Lincoln Tiberius James

About the Author

Lincoln T. James is a former stock broker and investment adviser. Voracious reader with interests in, and a focus on: investing, risk analysis, equities markets, retirement planning, 401k and IRAs, behavioral finance, economics, sales and marketing, e-commerce. When not reading you can find him golfing, fishing or gardening.

I really appreciate you taking the time to read my book! I hope you found the book valuable. Connect with me on social media. Also, I would like to ask a favor. If you liked the book, I would sure appreciate it if you could leave me a review on my book's page on Amazon.com.

Thanks ~ LTJ

Friend me on Facebook:
http://www.facebook.com/TheReluctantBull

Follow me on Twitter:
http://twitter.com/LTJ1959

ABOUT THE AUTHOR

Connect with me on LinkedIn:
https://www.linkedin.com/pub/lincoln-t-james/b5/221/3b8

Visit my website:
http://www.reluctantbull.com/.

Contact me by email:
lincolntjames@reluctantbull.com

Recommended Reading List

I have read all of these books and highly recommend them. They are in no particular order and no author has paid to have his work included here. If you are reading the digital version of this book, for your convenience, I have made the titles clickable links to the books on Amazon. If you are reading the print version of this book, links to these resources can be found on my website -

http://www.reluctantbull.com/gamblers-guide

Unexpected Returns: Understanding Secular Stock Market Cycles ~ by Ed Easterling

The New Market Wizards: Conversations with America's Top Traders ~ by Jack D. Schwager

Market Wizards: Interviews with Top Traders ~ by Jack D. Schwager

Stocks for the Long Run 5/E: The Definitive Guide to Financial Market Returns & Long-Term Investment Strategies ~ by Jeremy J. Siegel

RECOMMENDED READING LIST

Just One Thing: Twelve of the World's Best Investors Reveal the One Strategy You Can't Overlook ~ by John Mauldin

The Richest Man in Babylon ~ by George S. Clason

When to Sell: Inside Strategies for Stock-Market Profits ~ by Justin Mamis

How to Make Money in Stocks: A Winning System in Good Times and Bad ~ by William O'Neil

Buy High, Sell Higher: Why Buy-And-Hold Is Dead And Other Investing Lessons from CNBC's "The Liquidator" ~ by Joe Terranova

Stan Weinstein's Secrets For Profiting in Bull and Bear Markets ~ by Stan Weinstein

Fooled by Randomness: The Hidden Role of Chance in Life and in the Markets ~ by Nassim Nicholas Taleb

The Nature of Risk: Stock Market Survival and the Meaning of Life ~ by Justin Mamis

Irrational Exuberance ~ by Robert J. Shiller

Reminiscences of a Stock Operator ~ by Edwin Lefèvre

The Battle for Investment Survival ~ by Gerald M. Loeb

What I Learned Losing a Million Dollars ~ by Jim Paul

Dual Momentum Investing: An Innovative
Strategy for Higher Returns with Lower Risk - by
Gary Antonacci

Glossary

401k: Retirement investment account offered by your employer. Many of these accounts offer some sort of matched contribution by your employer. Always contribute at least to the amount matched by your employer.

AMEX: American Stock Exchange

Ask or offer: The price of a stock or option that the seller is willing to accept for selling a security. This is the price that you will pay to purchase the stock or option.

Alpha: A measure of performance. Compares the risk-adjusted performance of a mutual fund to a benchmark index. A positive alpha of 1.0 means that the fund has outperformed its benchmark index by 1%, a corresponding negative alpha would indicate an underperformance of 1%.

Beta: Beta represents a measure of volatility or an asset's risk in relation to the market as a whole.

Bear: Is an investor who believes that the market as a whole, or an individual stock price, will decline.

Bear Market: Market where prices are trending lower.

Bond: A debt instrument representing the debt of a company, municipality or the federal government. Long term security repaid to investors on a specified date. Bonds pay interest as regularly scheduled income with relatively low risk depending on their bond rating. Bonds offer attractive and regular returns for those living off of their investments.

Bull: Investor who believes that the market as a whole, or an individual stock price, will increase.

Bull Market: Market where prices are trending higher.

Diversification: Strives to limit your exposure to risk. Being overly concentrated in one market segment (example tech / dot com bubble) can expose you to substantial risk. Bottom line: don't put all your eggs in one basket.

Dividend: Usually a taxable income paid by a corporation as a portion of their earnings, based on profitability of the company, determined by the board of directors and paid as a cash payment to the individual investors on a per share basis.

Dividend Reinvestment Plan (DRIP): Companies allow dividends to be reinvested with no commission for additional common shares.

Equities: Stocks or security representing ownership interest.

ETFs: Exchange Traded Fund, trades on the stock exchange like a stock but the fund will hold assets. Many are tied to indexes. They differ from mutual funds in that they trade over the course of the day, where mutual funds only trade at end of business day closing price.

Exchange listed security: Securities admitted with full trading privileges on an exchange such as AMEX, NYSE and NASDAQ.

IRA: Individual retirement account. You can have either a traditional self-directed IRA or a ROTH IRA. These plans differ with regards to when you pay taxes. The Roth is funded with after tax dollars and your gains are not taxed when you take them out. The traditional IRA is funded with pre-tax dollars and the principle plus gains are taxed when you withdraw funds. Almost anyone with earned income can contribute to a traditional IRA. There are income limits to contribute to a ROTH. Read your plan's prospectus for full details.

Market Capitalization: Total dollar value of all outstanding shares issued by a corporation.

Market Index: Indexes present a summary of the market sector they represent. Examples of indexes include: S&P 500 is the Standard & Poor's 500, DJIA is the Dow Jones Industrial Average, the Willshire 5000, the Russell 2000.

Mutual Funds: Actively managed funds that charge a fee for their market management expertise. Trades are executed once a day using the end of business day closing price. These types of funds are a common offering in 401ks.

NASDAQ: National Association of Securities Dealers Automated Quotations. A stock exchange.

NYSE: New York Stock Exchange is the oldest stock exchange in the United States, founded in 1792.

P/E Ratio: The price of a stock relative to its earnings.

ROTH IRA: See IRA above.

S&P 500: Is an example of a market index. S&P 500 tracks 500 of the most widely held stocks on the NYSE and represents large cap companies across a broad sector.

Ticker / Symbol: The 3 to 5 letter designator for an investment vehicle. Example AMZN is the ticker symbol for Amazon.

Trailing Stop: A trailing stop order can protect your profits on a trade. The trailing stop is an exit point strategy for your trade. It is an automated way to sell your stock when conditions in the market change. You set up a trailing stop in advance which says sell this stock if the stock price falls by a preset percentage or dollar amount.

Yield: Ratio of how much a company's dividend is paying in relation to stock price. A measure of cash flow for each dollar invested in an equity position. If two companies are paying $1 per share and share prices are $20 and $40 then yields are 5% and 2.5% respectively. Your initial stock purchase price affects your yield as you own the security at a specific price.

Resources

Resource disclosure: Over the course of time website links may change. Every website here is independent and listed only as a convenience for the reader. The author receives no monetary benefit from these links being included. I do not endorse one company over any others that may be available. These are tools and websites that I use to research my own investments. Links were all verified and valid at time of publication in early 2015.

Big Charts: Stock charting website.

http://bigcharts.marketwatch.com/default.asp

Buyupside: Dividend Aristocrat list.

http://www.buyupside.com/dividendaristocrats/displayalldividendaristocrats.php

Comparison Traditional and Roth IRAs: US Government resource.

http://www.irs.gov/Retirement-Plans/Roth-Comparison-Chart

RESOURCES

Drip Investing: Dividend Champion list of companies that raised their dividends for 25 years or more. You can download an Excel Spreadsheet or pdf.

http://dripinvesting.org/tools/tools.asp

Dogs of the Dow: Website devoted to the Dogs of the Dow strategy. You can access the current list here.

http://www.dogsofthedow.com/

EODDATA: Website for end of day & historical stock data.

http://eoddata.com/splits.aspx

Get Split History: Stock split history data.

http://getsplith istory.com/

Investor Basics: US Government website resource.

http://www.investor.gov/investing-basics#.VKjUTSvF85s

Investor Compounding Calculator: US Government website resource.

http://www.investor.gov/tools/calculators/compound-interest-calculator#.VKZXWyvF85s

S&P 100 Constituents: Financial Times website allows you to see the list of stocks that comprise the S&P 100. Click the company name for specific financial data Example: yield, P/E...

http://markets.ft.com/research/Markets/Tearsheets/Constituents?s=OEX:MXP

84

S&P Dow Jones Indices: Multiple indexes offered by S&P.

http://us.spindices.com/

Yahoo Finance: Financial information website

http://finance.yahoo.com/

References

Barkley Rosser, Jr., J., Rosser, Marina V., and Gallegati, Mauro, A Minsky-Kindleberger Perspective On The Financial Crisis, January, 2012.

[DOC] from jmu.edu

http://cob.jmu.edu/rosserjb/A%20Minsky-Kindleberger%20Perspective%20on%20the%20Financial%20Crisis.docx

Ikenberry, David L. and Rankine, Graeme and Stice, Earl K., What Do Stock Splits Really Signal? *J. of Financial and Quantitative Analysis*, September 1996.

Available at SSRN:

http://ssrn.com/abstract=7929

Kahneman, Daniel, Knetsch, Jack L., and Thaler, Richard H., Anomalies: The Endowment Effect, Loss Aversion, and Status Quo Bias. *The Journal of Economic Perspectives*, Vol. 5, No. 1. (Winter, 1991), pp. 193-206.

Published by: American Economic Association

http://links.jstor.org/sici?sici=0895-3309%28199124%295%3A1%3C193%3AATEELA%3E2.0.CO%3B2-V

Kalay, Alon and Kronlund, Mathias, The Market Reaction to Stock Split Announcements: Earnings Information After All (May 10, 2014).

Available at SSRN:

http://ssrn.com/abstract=1027543 or http://dx.doi.org/10.2139/ssrn.1027543

Lakonishok, Josef and Smidt, Seymour, Are Seasonal Anomalies Real? A Ninety-Year Perspective. *The Review of Financial Studies* Vol. 1, No. 4 (Winter, 1988), pp. 403-425

Published by: Oxford University Press

http://www.jstor.org/stable/2962097

Silberberg, Alan et al. On Loss Aversion in Capuchin Monkeys. *Journal of the Experimental Analysis of Behavior* 89.2 (2008): 145–155. *PMC*. Web. 13 Feb. 2015.

Available at NCBI:

http://www.ncbi.nlm.nih.gov/pmc/articles/PMC2251327/

Study by the Staff of the U.S. Securities and Exchange Commission. Study Regarding Financial Literacy Among Investors August 2012

Available at http://www.sec.gov/

http://www.sec.gov/news/studies/2012/917-financial-literacy-study-part1.pdf

Tak Yan Leung, Oliver Meng Rui, and Steven Shuye Wanga, Do Stock Splits Really Signal? European Financial Management Association 2006 Annual Meetings

Available at http://www.efmaefm.org/

http://www.efmaefm.org/0EFMAMEETINGS/EFMA ANNUAL MEETINGS/2006-Madrid/papers/712910 full.pdf

Tuckett, David and Taffler, Richard, A Psychoanalytic Interpretation of Dot.com Stock Valuations (March 1, 2005).

Available at SSRN: http://ssrn.com/abstract=676635 or http://dx.doi.org/10.2139/ssrn.676635

Tversky, Amos and Kahneman, Daniel, Loss Aversion in Riskless Choice: A Reference-Dependent Model. *The Quarterly Journal of Economics*, Vol. 106, No. 4 (Nov., 1991), pp. 1039-1061

Published by: Oxford University Press

http://www.jstor.org/stable/2937956

Xu, Wei and McConnell, John J., Equity Returns at the Turn of the Month (July 2006).

Available at SSRN:

http://ssrn.com/abstract=917884Notes

Notes

LINCOLN T. JAMES

Notes

Notes

Notes

www.ingramcontent.com/pod-product-compliance
Lightning Source LLC
Chambersburg PA
CBHW021437170526
45164CB00001B/283